No Way Back

Helen Chapman
Illustrated by Warren Crossett

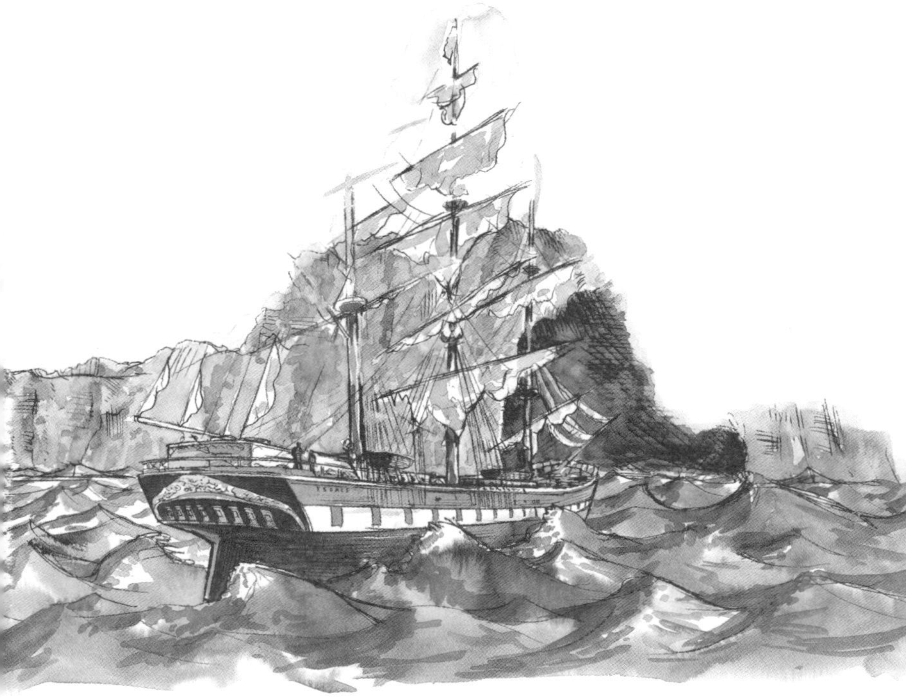

800-445-5985   www.etacuisenaire.com

No Way Back

ISBN 0-7406-1204-2
ETA 620041

ETA/Cuisenaire • Vernon Hills, IL 60061-1862
800-445-5985 • www.etacuisenaire.com

Published by ETA/Cuisenaire® under license from
Rigby Heinemann, a division of Reed International Books
Australia Pty Ltd. All rights reserved.

© Reed International Books Australia Pty Ltd 2001
Logo design © 2004 by ETA/Cuisenaire®

Text by Helen Chapman
Edited by Jay Dale
Text and cover designed by Catherine Squared Pty Ltd
Illustrated by Warren Crossett

No part of this publication may be reproduced, stored in a
retrieval system, or transmitted, in any form or by any means,
electronic, mechanical, photocopying, recording, or otherwise,
without the prior written permission of the publisher.

Printed in Hong Kong by Hing Yip Printing Limited

06 07 08 09 10 11 12 13   10 9 8 7 6 5 4 3 2

Contents

Prologue			5
Chapter 1	Labratory Rat		6
Chapter 2	I Haven't Been Born Yet!		10
Chapter 3	Trapped!		14
Chapter 4	The Giant Mouth		20
Chapter 5	To Sink Like a Stone		27
Chapter 6	Shipwrecked		33
Chapter 7	Stranded!		38
Chapter 8	So Much Gold		44
Chapter 9	Something Is Very Wrong		50
Chapter 10	The Sketch		58

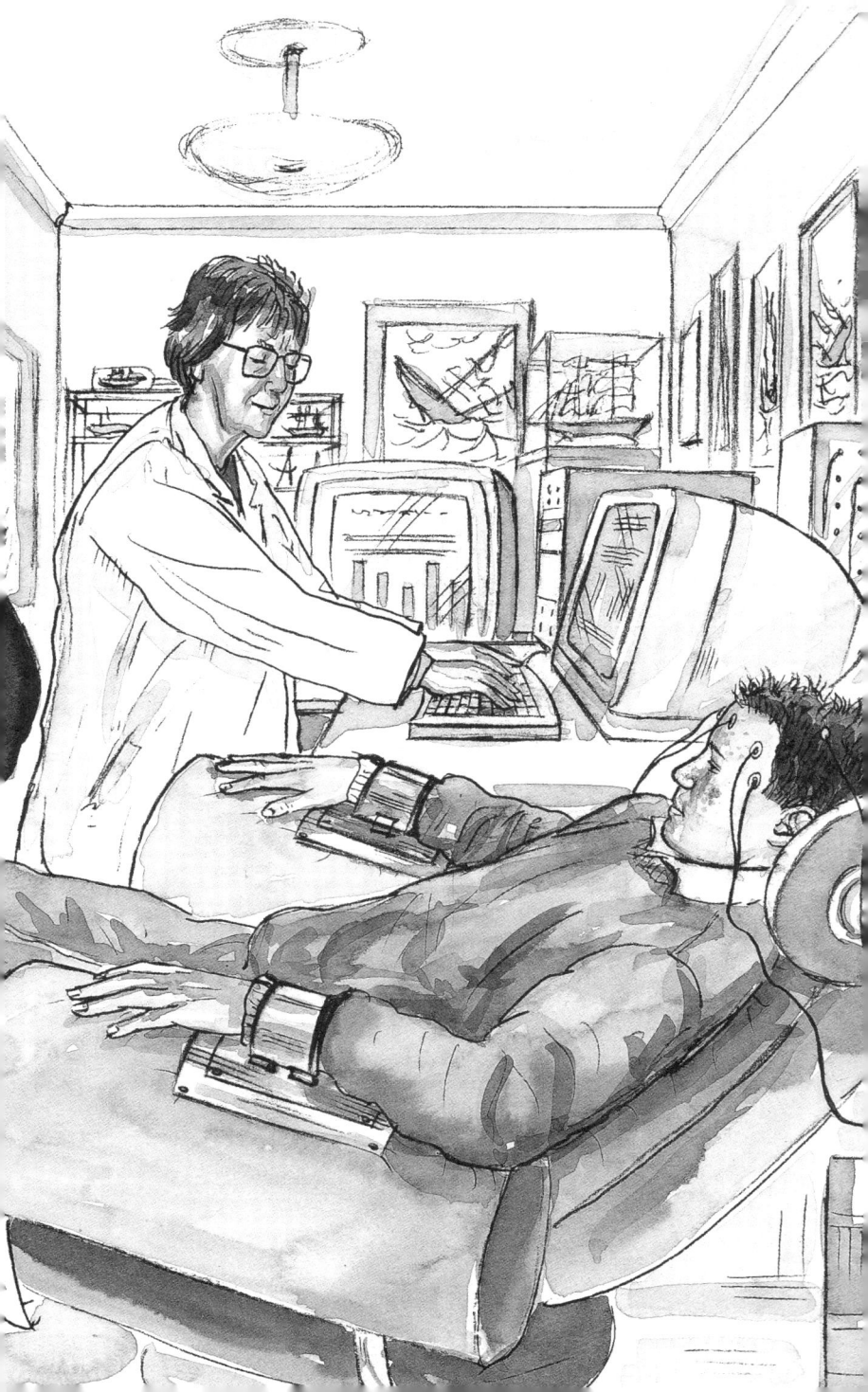

Prologue

Professor Maton never smiled. Today, however, she smiled not once, but twice. She smiled her first smile at the teenage boy strapped to a chair in her office. The second smile was at the virtual reality equipment attached to him. He wanted information on a shipwreck. Professor Maton needed to test her time travel program on a human "lab rat." Both were about to get what they wanted.

A siren wailed and the computer screen flashed. **WARNING! EMERGENCY! OVERLOAD!** Smoke billowed from the equipment. The professor kicked open the back panel. A waft of hot air and the pepper-like smell of charred wiring hit her in the face. Coughing from the fumes, she checked the wiring. The noise grew louder. The power went off, plunging the room into darkness and shutting down the equipment.

Professor Maton felt her way to the boy. He was not moving.

"No!" she screamed as she shook his body. "Don't die on me!"

Chapter 1

Labratory Rat

I had a loose thread in my sweater once. Little by little I pulled the thread, until the whole sleeve came off. My story's going to unravel just like that thread. It's about my trip back in time. And, no! I am not making this up. If I were, I'd make myself a hero, not a lab rat for a nutty professor whose experiment almost killed me!

I had been on a school trip that day. I knew that much. My class visited the Shipwreck Museum. I'd asked for information on the cargo ship the *Esdale* because my project was on it. The guide said that Professor Maton was an expert, and if she wasn't busy, I could see her.

Laboratory Rat

The guide took me into a room full of high-tech equipment. The professor said she'd written a virtual reality program about the *Esdale*. The problem was, data was missing. The *Esdale* had carried gold when it sank, but divers never found the wreck. By "plugging" me into her program, Professor Maton hoped I could find the gold.

She attached wires to my head and switched something on. A feeling like static clung to me, tingling my skin and setting my teeth on edge. A noise grew loud and sparks flew. The lights went off, and when I woke up, I was here.

"Here" was a room with worm-eaten walls and furniture. The room rocked and as I fell against a table—I realized I was on a ship.

"Cool program, Professor Maton," I said aloud, not knowing if she could hear me. "This table feels real."

The instruments and charts told me I was in the captain's cabin. A poster on the wall read "Sailing Orders for the *Esdale*, May 14th, 1866."

"No!" I shouted. "I don't believe it! This can't be the real *Esdale*."

Sudden stabs of pain spiked my forehead. A voice, magnified ten times over, filled the air.

"Mitch, can you hear me?"

I spun around. "Professor Maton?" I cried. "Where are you?"

The voice grew louder. I felt as if my mind was breaking into pieces, like a smashed mirror. The glass showed a different image in each piece. There was the Mitch back at the museum and another Mitch lost in a place full of shadows. But it was the third image that scared me the most. This Mitch could touch the wood of the ship. He could smell the salt of the sea. And he was lost—lost somewhere in time!

Chapter 2

I Haven't Been Born Yet!

The cabin started spinning, or was it me? I dropped to the floor. When the noise stopped, I realized the professor had moved me again. But where? All I could think of was a scary DVD I saw once. It was about the last man on Earth. He was all alone in a room... then there was a knock at his door! I, too, was afraid of being alone. But I was also afraid of what might be out there.

Slowly, I got to my feet... just as a voice spoke behind me. Something fleshy touched my arm. I screamed.

"Are you all right, boy?" asked a voice.

I turned to see a girl in a funny dress.

I Haven't Been Born Yet!

"No! Yes! Um, I guess so," I said, my heart thumping. "Where am I?"

"Here, of course," she said.

I glanced around a gloomy cabin. It was damp and smelled of mold. A flickering lamp showed a bunk and a bench. They were studded with nails and bolted to the floor.

"Where's here?" I asked.

The girl looked at me as if I were mad. "On the *Esdale* of course," she said.

"What's the year?" I asked, my voice trembling.

"It is eighteen sixty-six. What is wrong? Do you have the fever? My mama has, that is why she had to stay behind."

I flopped onto the hard bunk. Thanks to that nutty professor, I was stuck in the past. There had to be a way back. I needed to believe that, or I'd go mad.

"I don't belong here," I said.

"Are you on the wrong ship?" the girl asked. "We are sailing for England."

I felt sick. I knew the ship never made it that far. What was going to happen to me? Could I die before I'd been born?

"Papa went to see the captain," she chattered on. "He told me to sit quietly and sew. There was a loud noise and you appeared like magic. Can you do it again?"

I shook my head.

"My name is Amy Befeld," she said. "Do you have a name, boy?"

"I'm Mitch Tyler," I said. "Look, Amy, I don't belong here."

"I know!" Amy giggled. "This is a woman's cabin, so you must leave." She winked. "And so must I before I die from boredom."

Amy squashed her sewing into a battered leather traveling trunk. She went into the passageway. "Are you coming?"

There was no way I wanted to be on my own. What I did want was to be back in the museum. I followed Amy and found her bent over a gap in the decking.

"Look at this, boy," she said.

"Stop calling me that," I said crossly. "I'm older than you."

I crouched alongside her. We peered into the cargo hold. Inside it was almost black, but we could make out the shapes of hundreds of wool bales.

"What else is down there?" I asked, but not caring.

"Let's find out. Come on," Amy said. She scrunched up her long skirt, lay on her stomach, and wriggled backwards into the gap.

"Don't!" I begged. "Don't leave me!"

Amy didn't listen. Her head disappeared as she dropped. I grabbed for her arms, but I caught only air. There was a scream, a thud, and then nothing. Too scared to breathe, I peered into the hold.

"Amy?" I called. "Are you all right?"

There was no answer. The cargo hold was quiet, deathly quiet.

Chapter 3

Trapped!

"Amy!" I shouted. "Are you there?"

A voice drifted up. "Of course I am! Where else would I be? Hurry up."

I worked myself through the gap and dropped several yards onto a bale. Using the bale's straps, I climbed down. The only light trickled in from the gap above.

A sudden squeal made me jump.

"What was that?" Amy asked, her face bobbing up in front of me.

"I ... I don't know," I answered. "A rat, or something, I guess."

"I would rather it be the 'or something' than a rat," said Amy. "Can we go?"

"If you want," I said calmly. Truth was,

Trapped!

I was dead scared of rats. But there was no way would I let Amy know that.

I looked up and knew we had a problem. We couldn't get out! Even if we could climb to the top of the bales, we'd be yards away from the gap.

The same thought crossed Amy's mind. "Is it better to starve to death," she asked slowly, "or eat rats and die from disease?"

Above us, loud thuds echoed from the deck. Someone was coming! I began to shout, but I found Amy's hand across my mouth.

"The hold is out of bounds," she hissed. "They will lock us in the brig and then put us off at the next port. Papa will be so angry!"

The *Esdale* was my only link to the professor. If I left it, she might never find me.

"Okay," I said. "We'll hide; then we'll sneak out when we can."

Up high, the main hatch opened. The glow from a swinging lantern cast creeping shadows around. We saw a ladder and heard each rung creak under the weight of heavy boots. Three people squeezed between the towering maze of wool bales. They stopped near us.

"I have goldminers on board," said a man in uniform. "They have trusted me to keep their gold safe. Look!" He shone his lantern over a hollowed-out bale.

Amy and I blinked, trying to get used to the sudden light.

"Pardon me, Capt'n Hopping," said a sailor. A jagged, red scar ran from somewhere under a filthy bandana. It went down his forehead and across his pock-marked cheek. A gold front tooth showed out from a mouth full of yellow teeth. "But what be stopping ye taking me bag of gold dust?"

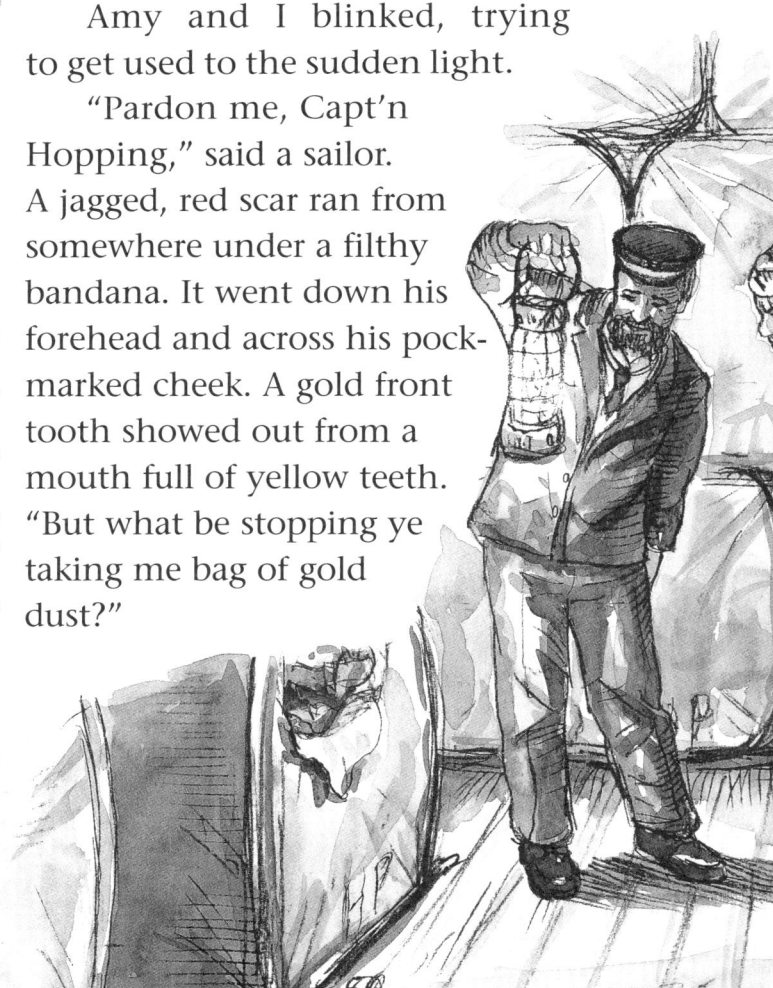

Trapped!

Captain Hopping laughed. "As you know, my official cargo is wool. However, I secretly loaded chests of gold to take to the Royal Mint in England. My cargo is worth over two million pounds. Your gold is but a trinket."

A third man came into view. "Gentlemen, I too have struck it rich," he said.

Amy gasped. "It is Papa!" She moved toward him, but I pulled her back.

"Wait," I hissed, "I need to hear about the gold."

The captain sensed movement and glanced over his shoulder. "Must be rats," he said.

The men put their bags of gold in the bale.

"Are you sure the hold is safe?" asked Amy's father.

Captain Hopping nodded.

"Cunning pirates might be on board," he replied. "My cabin is the first place they would look. But a hold filled with wool? How could they find one bale among hundreds?"

"Aye, how could they?" agreed the sailor.

He laughed quietly and picked at his gold tooth with a dirty fingernail.

Captain Hopping turned away. The men followed him to the ladder.

"All hatches into this hold are locked," he said. "Sailor, lock this one when we leave."

Amy and I had hoped to follow them out and not be seen. We started to move when a rat, the size of a football, sat upright, blocking our escape. Trapped again!

"Filthy thing," hissed Amy. "Get rid of it, Mitch."

Fear tickled the hair on my neck. I hated rats at the best of times, and this was not the best of times.

"Do something!" cried Amy.

"Like what?" I asked.

"Oh! You are such a baby," Amy said. She kicked at the rat. It squealed in rage as her boot made contact. The rat hit against my leg and clawed up my body. It stopped at my shoulder. My body shook as its whiskers twitched against my skin.

"Get out of here," I growled as I pushed it to the floor.

Trapped!

The sliver of light disappeared as the hatch slammed shut.

Amy screamed. "Papa! Wait!" But the bales muffled her voice.

I pulled myself onto a bale and scrambled across the top until I had passed the rat. Dropping to the floor, I felt my way to the ladder. I hauled myself up the rungs made sharp with scales of rust. Reaching the hatch, I thumped as hard as I could.

"Help! Let us out!"

Way down below, I heard Amy sob.

"Oh, Mitch! What will we do?"

Chapter 4
The Giant Mouth

The hatch was too heavy to push open, so I peered through the cracks ready to shout when someone walked past. Time passed with the speed of a sick turtle. Finally, I heard footsteps. They stopped above me, and the hatch opened. I saw a cutlass and dirty boots. Something wasn't right. I scrambled down.

"Hide," I said.

"No!" said Amy. "Getting into trouble is better than starving."

Before I could explain, legs backed down the ladder. As soon as she could, Amy flung her arms around the man's waist.

The Giant Mouth

"Eh, who be that?"

Startled, he swung round and lowered his lamp. His gold tooth shone in the light. Amy screamed. She was hugging the man with the scar.

Amy thought quickly.

"Oh sir, thank goodness you found me. I was exploring and got shut in by mistake," she stammered.

He pushed Amy up the ladder. "Be gone," he said. "And if ye speak of seeing me, I be slicing ye to ribbons."

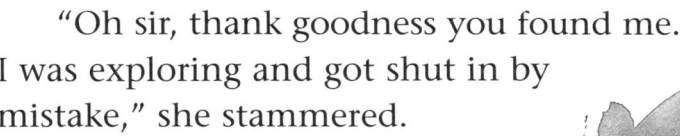

Amy fled up the ladder. The man disappeared among the bales. I heard gold nuggets clinking as he grabbed the bags.

Quickly, I came out of my hiding place and slipped up the ladder without being seen. Amy was waiting for me. Her mouth was a tight line as she tried not to cry.

"Hurry!" she said, grabbing my arm. "We must get back to my cabin."

"No way!" I said. "You have to tell your dad about that guy."

"No!" Amy cried. "He will kill me if I tell." She burst into tears.

"But he's stealing the gold!" I shouted.

"He cannot go anywhere!" Amy shouted back. "I shall tell Papa just before we reach port, all right?"

"No!" I said. "I'm going to tell Captain Hopping." And I stormed off.

When I got to the upper-deck, I realized I couldn't tell the captain. I was a stowaway, and he might lock me up.

What I needed to do was to get my hands on some gold. Then Professor Maton would bring me back—I was sure of it.

The Giant Mouth

The deck was shrouded in fog, and I felt like a fly trapped in a giant web. A sailor strode by shouldering a coil of rope. Sweat poured from his face, covering it in a salty sheen.

NO WAY BACK

With one movement, he swung the rope onto the deck and thumped me on my arm. "I be Zilla."

He thumped me so roughly that his golden earrings shook.

"I be, I mean, I am Mitch, Mitch Tyler."

"Be listening," he said.

"To what?" I asked.

"The wind," said Zilla. "She been and dropped."

I peered up through the thick fog. The sails wrapped around the masts and sagged limply like wet spaghetti.

"So?" I shrugged.

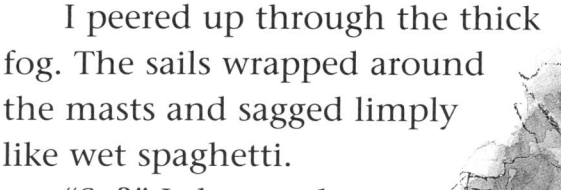

The Giant Mouth

"Land lubber," sighed Zilla. "Without wind, our sails be useless. The currents here be dragging us toward the cliffs, to smash the *Esdale* to pieces."

A bell rang frantically, causing a frenzy of noise and activity.

"Rocks dead ahead!" cried the lookout.

Sailors scurried as the ship lurched and dipped like a roller coaster. The currents played with the *Esdale* as if it were a toy boat. I clutched a rail and threw up as dark cliffs loomed before the ship.

"Can Captain Hopping drop anchor and stop us drifting?" I asked nervously.

"The sea be too deep," said Zilla. "Come, help uncoil this rope. We be needing it before too long."

The scratchy rope was very heavy. I needed both arms to move it. In the grayness came a grinding crash as the *Esdale* struck the rocks. With a sickening crunch, the rudder smashed. All control of the ship was lost to human hands. I was flung across the deck.

"Professor Maton!" I screamed. "Get me out of here!"

A series of crashes and groans followed as the ship scraped alongside the cliff face. I screamed as a giant mouth in the cliff face yawned before us. The ship was being forced toward the mouth, and there was nothing anybody could do to stop it. We were all about to die!

Chapter 5
To Sink Like a Stone

The current sucked the ship inside the cave. The noise was deafening as the waves boomed and echoed. I was petrified, but Captain Hopping and the crew knew what to do. They calmly lowered two small boats into the water.

By now, most of the passengers were huddled on deck.

"Are we going in those boats?" Amy asked as she came alongside me.

"No," I said. "They're so the crew can inspect the damage."

Amy peered up into the darkness. "The mast is jammed under the roof of the cave. We are stuck!" she said.

NO WAY BACK

We had to wait ages for the tide to fall. As the sea level dropped, the main mast came free. I thought everything was okay until Amy's dad ran up.

"What's the matter, Papa?" Amy asked.

To Sink Like a Stone

He didn't answer. All color left his face. His hands gripped Amy's shoulders so tightly that his veins and bones stuck out. As the water ebbed and flowed, the *Esdale* was being sucked further inside. The roof of the cave got lower and the mast scraped against it. We ducked as rocks smashed onto the deck.

Finally, the mast jammed in the roof of the cave. The seesaw action of the sea began to break up the ship. Water poured in and the deck planks split. At first, there was no panic. I think everyone was too shocked. Then people dove overboard. They tried to swim to the boats, but the rough seas were deadly.

Amy's dad scooped her up. "Make for the longboat!" he yelled to me.

People were already inside it.

"Hey, matey!" said one of the sailors. "Pass me the girl. I be looking after her for ye." A smile spread across his cruel lips.

Amy squirmed in her father's arms as he carefully lowered her into the longboat into the arms of the man with the scar! Amy trembled as she took her seat beside him. The gold tooth flashed. "Looks like we be shipmates," he whispered. "I be watching every move ye make now. And so be me matey." He jerked his head toward the stern. I stared in disbelief. His "matey" was Zilla!

To Sink Like a Stone

I climbed into the longboat. We sat, silent and in near darkness, waiting for the *Esdale* to sink so we could untie the ropes and float off. But it all went wrong. The longboat began to fill with sea water. We tried to scoop it out with our hands, but it flooded in too fast. We all worked frantically as there was so little time. Then there was no time at all. Within seconds, the boat tipped over. Ice-cold water flooded in, and we were washed overboard.

Inky black water swirled fiercely about me. The boat sank like a stone and sucked me down. I let out a great breath, sank, and drew in my next breath underwater. Coughing and spluttering, I pushed upwards. I couldn't believe this was happening. I should be at the museum, not drowning.

"Professor Maton!" I gasped as I reached the surface. "Help me!"

Chapter 6

shipwrecked

The screams of people choked the air, but somehow Amy heard me. We clung to a deck plank and looked around for her dad. People thrashed about in the waves, but most were not strong enough to fight against the icy water and the weight of their heavy clothes. One by one, they went under.

After a while, an eerie calm hung over the cave. My last memory of the *Esdale* was of Captain Hopping. He stood on the rigging waving a handkerchief, as he went down with his ship.

"We must get out of the cave," yelled Amy. "Or the *Esdale* will suck us down."

I knew she was right—I'd seen *Titanic*! But no way was I letting go of the plank.

"Professor Maton," I cried. "I want out!"

Amy must have thought I was nuts. "Stay calm, Mitch," she begged.

I knew we had to reach the smaller boats outside the cave, but I didn't know how. Amy must have read my mind.

"Pretend I am racing you," she suggested. "Swim across the currents, not against them."

I knew she'd never make it in all that clothing. "Amy! Get out of your skirt and petticoats," I said. "They'll drag you under."

Amy undid the buttons around her waist. She swam off, leaving a swirl of clothing floating behind her. I let go of the plank. Water splashed my face, making me struggle for every breath. I matched my strokes to Amy's as we fought through the waves. We finally swam through the cave mouth. The boats looked so far away that I didn't think I could make it. The people on the boats must have felt the same. They rowed closer and pulled us in with boat hooks.

Shipwrecked

"We're safe, Amy!" I cried as we collapsed on the floor.

Amy's face turned such a deadly white that I thought she would faint. What could be more scary than a shipwreck? I followed her gaze—and saw the man with the scar!

Our desperate voyage to find land was unreal. After the first day, I don't really remember much. It passed in a dream from being here to being back in the Shipwreck Museum. I could even see flashing lights and hear a voice calling to me to come back.

After a few days, we found land and scrambled ashore. Half-frozen, dazed and exhausted, we collapsed on the rocks. Gulls were circling in a gray haze when I opened my eyes. My mouth tasted of salt, and my lips were cracked and bleeding.

"Amy?" I tried to call, but could only groan.

The island was bleak and swept by winds and rain. I sat up stiffly, hurting everywhere when I tried to move. I looked over to see Amy half walking, half crawling along the beach. She had purple circles under her eyes, and her hair was tangled around her face.

"Wait up, lass," said a man. "You are going the wrong way. Make for the hut. You too, lad. My name is Bosun Rowan, and I will look after you."

He led us away from the beach. There, on a bald hill, was an old whalers' hut. We staggered inside and were covered instantly in spider webs that hung like fishing nets across the hut. Cold air snuck in between the gaps in the walls and between the cracks of the boarded-up window. Amy and I huddled together.

Moments later, another bedraggled group of survivors entered. Amy never took her eyes off the man with the scar. When he saw her staring, he gave an ugly grin. With lightning speed, he pulled his cutlass free. Its blade was a blur of flashing steel as he slashed at the air in front of Amy.

Chapter 7

Stranded!

Bosun Rowan grabbed the sailor by the arm. "Are you mad?" he yelled. "Put that thing away or I will have you keelhauled." He forced the cutlass to the ground and sat back down.

"He wants to kill me," Amy sobbed.

"Nay, lass," said the bosun. "Bernadin is only showing off. Likes to think he is a pirate with that scar of his. Truth is, he is a wily sailor like the rest of us."

He saw the fear still in Amy's face. "Come here. You too, lad."

We sat by him, and he put his strong arms around us. "Sleep," he said gently.

Stranded!

From time to time, Bosun Rowan would mechanically give our heads a rub with his rough hands. Warmed by his body and safe from Bernadin, Amy and I fell asleep.

When morning came, the bosun took charge. "To stay alive, we must share everything," he said. "Now, what have you all got?"

Among us, we had a few tins of soup and one wax match. Not much to keep fifteen people alive.

"Zilla, Bernadin, take six men and see what food you can find," he ordered. "The rest of you, come with me and collect timber."

We found dry timber and made a woodpile under the shelter of a tree. Crew members made a circle to act as a windbreak. The bosun took our only match and knelt down. He struck the match, it lit, and the timber caught fire.

"That match is more use to us than all the gold on board the *Esdale*," whispered Amy.

"Not to me, it isn't," I thought.

Amy was right about the match, though. The fire kept us warm, cooked our food, and was a signal to any passing ships.

During the long days, the men hunted seals and wild pigs. Amy and I helped to make rough clothes from the skins. We also used seal skins to patch up the gaps in the hut walls and floor. I kept an eye on Bernadin and Zilla but never saw any clue as to where the gold was. They must have hidden it, but where? I needed to know.

Stranded!

Our lives turned into one endless nightmare. The shock of being caught up in something that happened over one hundred years ago had gone. My home, the Shipwreck Museum, and the *Esdale* were like a dream. I had work to do every day, just to stay alive. I felt so depressed that I gave up caring about the gold.

After weeks of cold and hunger, Bosun Rowan left. He took three men and sailed away to try to get help.

"I want him back," sobbed Amy. "I want Papa back. Nothing is fair."

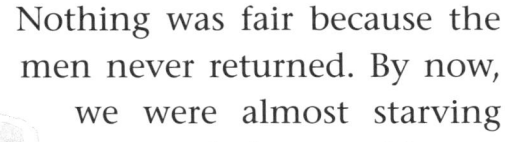

Nothing was fair because the men never returned. By now, we were almost starving and always cold.

Then, one day, a change.

"A ship!" cried a voice. "A ship!"

We stood by the fire and waved as a ship drew near. Amy stopped waving and looked around.

"What's wrong?" I asked.

"Where are Bernadin and Zilla?"

"Who cares?" I laughed. "Amy! We're saved!"

"I care," she said as she stormed off. "The stolen gold belongs to the families of the people who drowned."

"We can't prove a thing!" I shouted.

Amy didn't listen. She went looking for them and, of course, I followed. We found them easily. With all the excitement, they knew no one would be interested in them. They didn't reckon on Amy! Zilla was scraping away dirt from a hole, while Bernadin dragged small bags from their hiding place.

"Fools they be," said Bernadin, "who think all the gold went down with the *Esdale*."

"Aye, 'twas a scurvy theft we made," laughed Zilla.

Bernadin weighed the bags in his hands and tossed half to Zilla.

"This be your share, matey," he said. He got to his feet and walked off. "Let us be picking the seas clean of more gold."

Zilla rose slowly. He drew out a knife from his seal-skin belt.

"Why does he need that?" whispered Amy nervously.

Zilla turned and stared at us, his knife pointed in our direction. For seconds the world stood still as our eyes met. Amy and I waited in silence to be killed.

Chapter 8

So Much Gold

A smile spread across Zilla's face. He touched the hilt of his knife to his chin in the old pirate's salute and then put it back in his belt.

"I like the cut of your jib," he said in a grave whisper. "Good luck to ye, lad."

He tossed one bag to us, then vanished. The bag fell at our feet.

"That is Papa's bag," said Amy quietly. "Look! I sewed his name on it."

I was so stunned at still being alive that I just stood there. Amy picked up the bag. She opened it and trickled the gold nuggets through her fingers.

"So much gold!" she said tearfully. "Poor Papa must have worked very hard."

So Much Gold

"I know, Amy," I said. "But think of his excitement at finding it."

We walked back to the beach. Zilla was waist-deep in water shaking the hand of a sailor in a whaleboat.

"She be the whaler *Helena*," he yelled, pointing to the anchored ship. "She be taking us home."

Zilla saw me watching. He put a finger to his lips, as if to stop me saying anything that might get him into trouble with Bernadin. I understood and saluted him. He gave a big laugh and saluted back.

"Really, Mitch," sighed Amy. "How can you like that horrid man?"

The *Helena* set sail for New Zealand. Our voyage was normal, apart from one strange thing. One night, as we anchored to ride out a storm, one whaleboat went missing. Zilla and Bernadin were missing, too! And with them went the gold.

When we arrived in the port of Dunedin, people stared at us bug-eyed. With our rough skin and tattered seal-skin clothes, we looked like wild things. I kept looking for the television reporters and camera crews!

NO WAY BACK

There weren't any, just reporters wearing suits and hats. We told our story. An artist even sketched Amy for the newspaper!

Right away, men set out to try to find the shipwreck. Everyone knew about the gold. We thought it was a big secret. What they didn't know was that pirates were on board. No one believed us when we told them.

Amy and I were too sick and weak to do anything. The gold nuggets meant we had enough money to stay in a guest house. So eating, sleeping, and hanging around were what we did. A police officer gave us a telegraph message sent by Amy's mom. She was sailing out on the next ship. Then she and Amy would sail on to England.

Amy read part of her mom's message aloud. "I am bringing a surprise—a man who is now dear to my heart. He too was shipwrecked."

"Mitch," said Amy excitedly. "Do you think she means Bosun Rowan?"

"I don't know," I said. "Shipwrecks and rescues happen all the time. We'll have to wait and see."

With every month, Amy's excitement to see her mom grew. I was nervous. I hoped Mrs. Befeld would take me, too. I had nowhere else to go.

Finally, we stood at the docks waiting to see her.

"There she is!" Amy shouted. She forced her way along the crowded pier and waited by the gangplank. "But who is that man holding her hand?"

By going up closer, I could have seen his face. I didn't go up closer. I didn't need to. I knew.

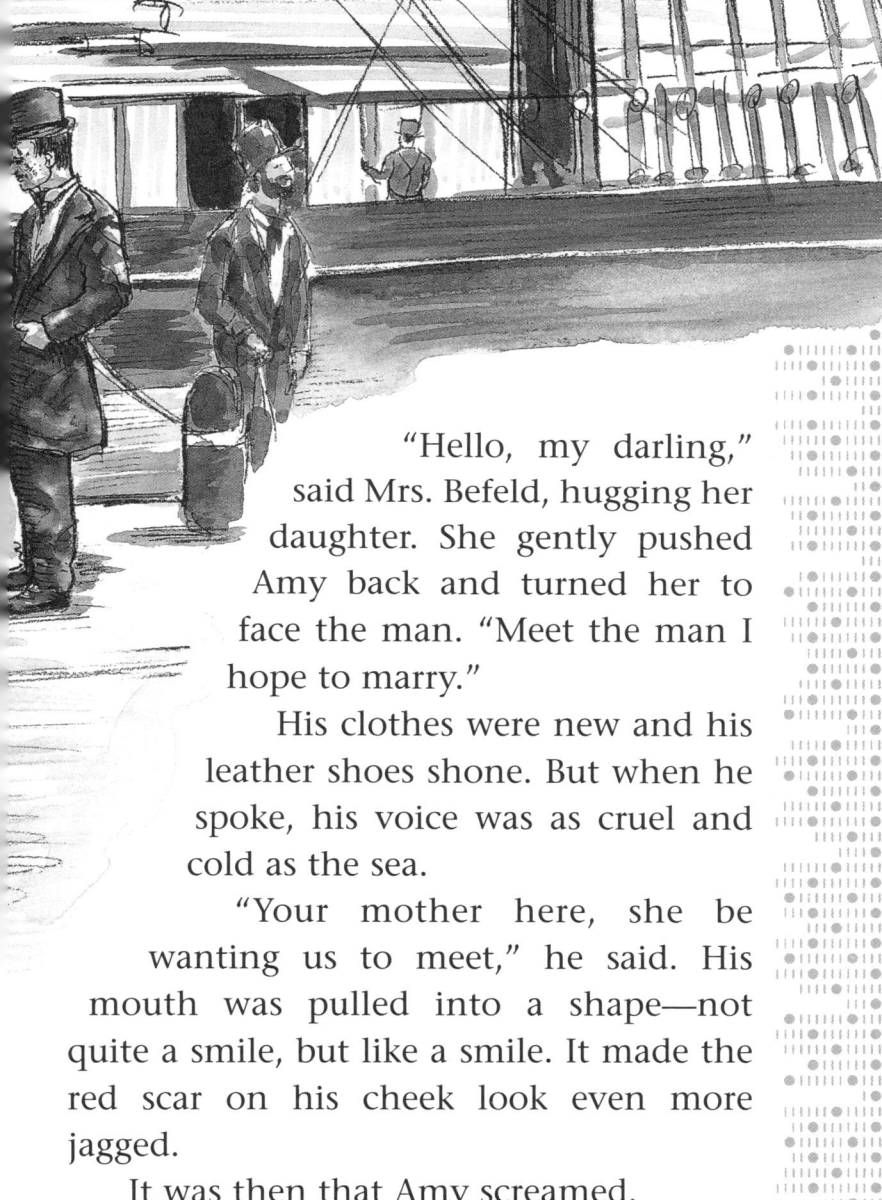

"Hello, my darling," said Mrs. Befeld, hugging her daughter. She gently pushed Amy back and turned her to face the man. "Meet the man I hope to marry."

His clothes were new and his leather shoes shone. But when he spoke, his voice was as cruel and cold as the sea.

"Your mother here, she be wanting us to meet," he said. His mouth was pulled into a shape—not quite a smile, but like a smile. It made the red scar on his cheek look even more jagged.

It was then that Amy screamed.

Chapter 9
Something Is Very Wrong

I tried to run toward Amy, but I couldn't move. I felt dizzy. I closed my eyes for a moment, drawing a few deep breaths to try to clear my head. Cold sweat ran down my back. I brushed a hand across my forehead, and it came away wet. Something was very wrong.

"Amy?" I said weakly. I opened my eyes and blinked. I felt a new wave of dizziness, but this one was caused by shock. Amy and everything else was gone!

I stared at the scene that met my eyes, without believing it. I was back in Professor Maton's office! I don't know why, but the sight of her filled me with horror.

Something Is Very Wrong

"Oh no!" I whimpered.

Shock rooted me to the chair. I turned so sick and cold that I thought I was going to pass out.

"Amy? What's happened to Amy?" I shouted.

Professor Maton shrugged as she undid the straps.

"No one's here, but us," she said. "What about the gold? Did you find it?"

I could not believe this woman!

"Yeah, I found it," I said. "Look, how long has it been since you put these on me?" I ripped off the wires. "I went into the past, didn't I? Where's it all gone? Where's Amy and her mom and Bernadin? How did I get back here?"

"Back where?" demanded Professor Maton. "What's the matter with you? You've never left this room."

Too much was happening too quickly. Suddenly, I started to laugh. I suppose, when everything is piled on top of you, you have to laugh.

Professor Maton peered over her glasses at me. "Don't get hysterical," she said. "What's wrong?" Her hand reached for my arm, but I pulled back.

"Were you experimenting with time?" I asked.

I heard my voice getting shrill, but I couldn't stop it. I felt as if I'd stepped through a doorway from the real world into an empty space, and I was falling through it. The silly thing was that I was back in my own time, and I was safe. I could go home as if nothing had happened. But something had happened. I'd met Amy, and I couldn't just leave her—not with Bernadin! All that time with her was lost, and I never even said goodbye. I couldn't stop the helpless trickle of tears.

Professor Maton helped me to stand up.

Something Is Very Wrong

"The equipment had a short circuit," she said. "It caused a glitch in my program. Instead of stopping, the program kept running. It runs on data I fed into it, but it appears to have fed off your thoughts, as well. Amazing!"

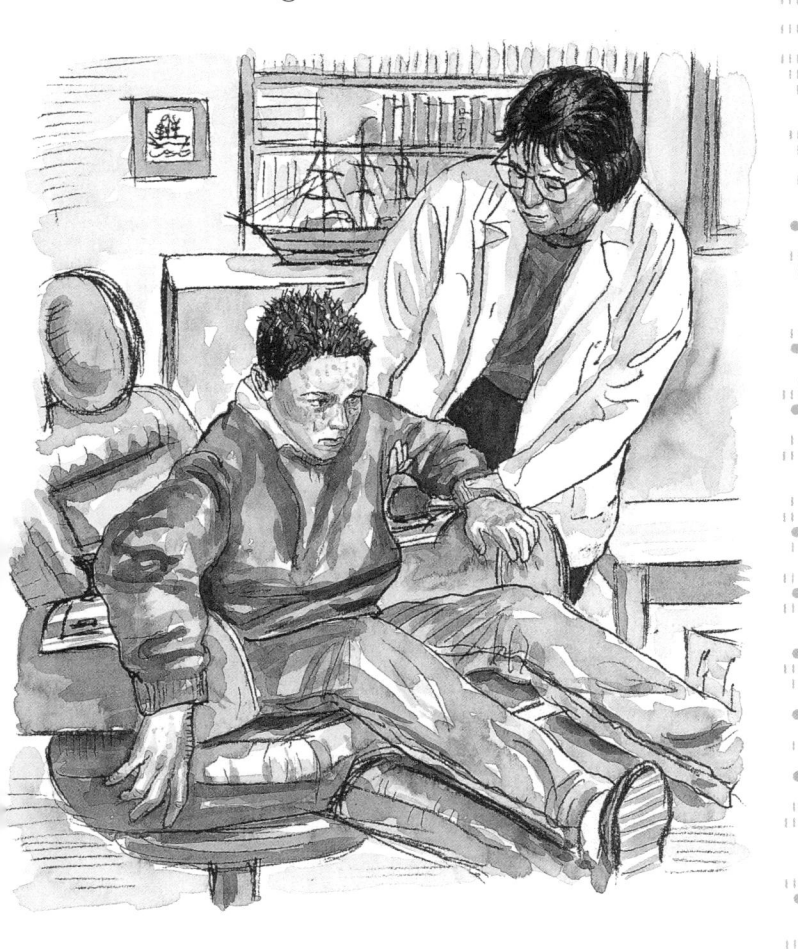

She started to program data into her computer. "Tell me about the lost gold. Then you can go."

I looked at the computer. It was eleven o'clock. Only a couple of hours had passed since I first came into the professor's office!

"Hang on," I said. "I'm trying to work out what's happened. One minute I was on the docks in eighteen sixty-six. The next thing I know, I'm here."

Something Is Very Wrong

Professor Maton looked up from the computer screen.

"Hmm. What? Oh, yes. My program is brilliant, isn't it? It was all an illusion."

"Was it? It was so real." I stopped. I didn't want to say anything else. I already felt stupid enough.

"I could taste the salt on my lips, feel the icy seas," I said quietly.

"You experienced the past without having left this room," said Professor Maton.

I stared at my clothes; they obviously weren't from the 1860s.

"But a virtual reality program can only do what it's programmed to do, right?" I said.

"Not when it's my program!" Professor Maton said proudly. "Mine searches for information. I knew there was gold, but not where it was. So, did you find it?"

She grabbed me by the shoulders. "Look, we both got what we wanted. You learned about a shipwreck, and I tested my program. I'm sorry about the glitch. The back-up should have come on quicker than it did. Now, tell me about the gold."

"There was gold," I said. "Pirates named Bernadin and Zilla stole what they could carry. The rest sank with the *Esdale* in a cave."

I had an idea as to how to see Amy again. "Why don't we try again?" I suggested. "I could get more information for you."

"There's no need," Professor Maton said. "I can trace those names easily; they're both unusual."

She picked up her cell phone. "I'll head up a search in the cave. Divers have looked before and not found anything. But there was never proof the gold was on the ship. I have proof now."

Professor Maton propelled me toward the door. "You'd better be going. Your teacher was looking for you before," she said. "I told her you were doing research with me."

I walked like a robot down the corridor and into the main area. My teacher was ordering kids out of the museum shop and onto the bus. By the time I got on, the only spare seat was by my teacher, or a girl from another class. I chose the girl. I glanced

Something Is Very Wrong

down at the clipboard on her lap and froze. Under the clip was a photocopy of an old newspaper sketch ... of Amy!

Chapter 10
The Sketch

I started to say something, but my voice dried up. All I could do was point a shaking finger at the sketch. After a long moment, I finally spoke.

"Who's the sketch of?"

The girl turned to me, surprised that I was interested.

"My great-grandmother, Amy Befeld," she said. "My project's on the *Esdale*. Amy was the only kid to survive the shipwreck."

"No, she wasn't," I said without thinking. "I did,..." My voice trailed to a mumble. "...too."

The Sketch

The girl scooped up the clipboard and hugged it tightly. "You're making fun of me!"

She turned away so quickly that her long hair slapped me in the face.

"Oh, Amy," I said softly. "You were real."

I turned toward the girl, wishing I could remember her name. "I am interested, honest. It just came out wrong," I said. "I'm doing my project on the *Esdale*, too. I thought there were more kids on board, that's all. Can I see the sketch again, please?"

My saying "please" made her turn. Her eyes narrowed into little slits as she glared at me. Without a word, she gave me the sketch.

"This was done in Dunedin," I said. "Before Bernadin came back."

The girl caught her breath. "How do you know that?" she asked.

"I know a lot about what happened," I said. "Look! I've got an idea. Do you want to work with me on the project? By the way, my name's Mitch."

"Yeah, I know. I'm Olivia," said the girl. "I don't mind working with you. I know about Amy, of course. But not much else. So don't say I didn't warn you."

"What happened to her?" I asked. "Was she happy?"

"Happy? That's a funny thing to ask," Olivia said. "I suppose she was. Her mother married this guy Bernadin after Amy's dad drowned in the shipwreck. They lived in London and had heaps of money. You know, nice house, servants, that sort of thing. Bernadin wasn't around much. He loved the sea and was always off having adventures."

"I bet he was," I said. Still, it seemed like Amy had done okay.

Olivia opened her clipboard and sorted through some notes. "Amy got married in eighteen seventy-two," she read. "She had two boys, Mitch and Tyler. Funny names, aren't they? I mean for back then. Boys usually had names like Edward or Charles."

Two things happened then to spook me. The first was hearing the names, my names. The second was the look of shock

The Sketch

on Olivia's face when I gave back the sketch. Her hand fell away, and at first, she didn't speak. Her face grew confused and her eyes darted from the sketch to my eyes. And back again.

"The boy in the background looks like you," she said quietly. A look of worry crept across her face. She guessed something was weird, but she couldn't figure out what.

"This is so like you," she continued. She bit her lip. "He even has the same funny pattern of freckles across his cheek."

Still, Olivia couldn't accept the crazy truth.

"No, you couldn't have met Amy," she said. "It's not possible. But facts are facts. You knew Bernadin's name. That's one fact. You're in this newspaper sketch. That's another. And, one of Amy's sons has a modern name, your name. That's three facts."

What I should have done was say nothing, but I couldn't help myself. "You're wrong," I said. "It's four facts. Two of Amy's sons have modern names. I didn't tell you, but my last name is Tyler."

Olivia shifted nervously. She sat thinking and waiting for everything to make sense. Her lips were open a bit, as if she wanted to speak but couldn't find the words.

"This is too weird," she said after a while. "Want to tell me about it?"

My mind raced a dozen different ways, none of them toward a way out of this.

The Sketch

In the end, I thought about what I would think if someone told me such a story.

"I'm going to write it down first," I said, "before I forget. You can read it later, if you want."

Olivia looked at me, started to say something, then gave up. We sat in silence until the bus pulled up in front of our school. Then, while we shuffled along the aisle, she spoke.

"I'd like to read your story," she said.

We piled out of the bus as Olivia kept talking. "Tell you what, Mom's put all our old photos onto disk. Do you want to come over on the weekend? I'll see what we can find on Amy."

"Cool," I said. "It'll have to be Sunday, okay? I need to do something at the Shipwreck Museum on Saturday."

I walked into my classroom and thought about Saturday morning. Professor Maton didn't know it yet, but she was going to get another chance to test her virtual reality program.